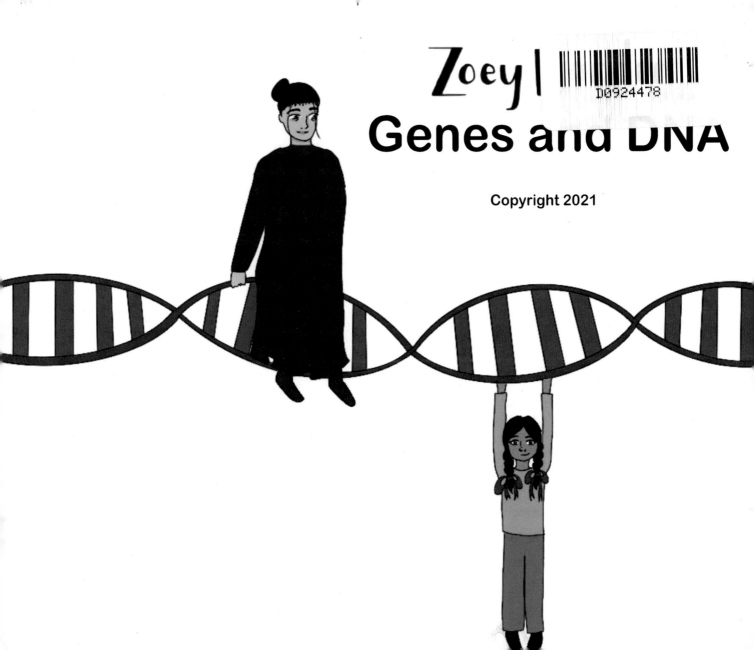

Zoey | Genes and DNA

Copyright 2021

One morning, as Zoey was brushing her teeth, she looked up into the mirror. She noticed her dark brown eyes, her long straight hair, her light brown skin. And she began to wonder as questions popped into her head:

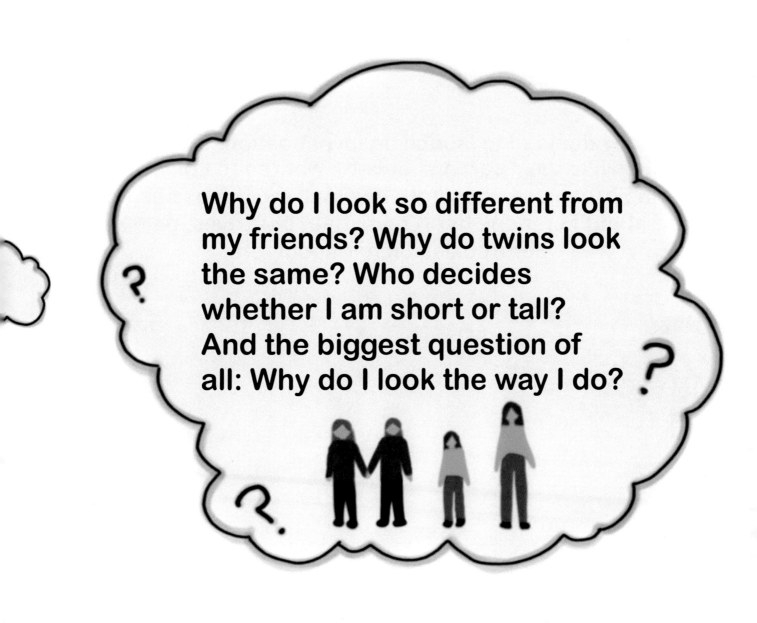

So Zoey decided to launch an investigation. She knew kids looked like their parents, but she wanted to know more. During breakfast, she wrote down all the things she could see about her mom: her blonde hair, blue eyes, pale skin, her freckles on her shoulders.

After school, she wrote down all the things she could see about her dad: his mustache, his beard, his black hair and brown eyes. She put the lists together and, remembering what she looked like, thought one thing: It doesn't add up!

During dinner, she decided to ask her parents. "What makes me look like you?" She questioned. "And who decides which parts of you I get?" "I'm not sure, honey," they said. "That's just genetics."

But Zoey just kept wondering. What was genetics? How did it work? Before she went to bed she wrote a third list about herself. She hung the lists up beside her bed and went to sleep still wondering.

When Zoey opened her eyes, she was shocked and amazed by the place around her. She was standing on a long string of DNA that looped and waved and spun into the distance on both sides of her. It was like a long, bendy ladder!

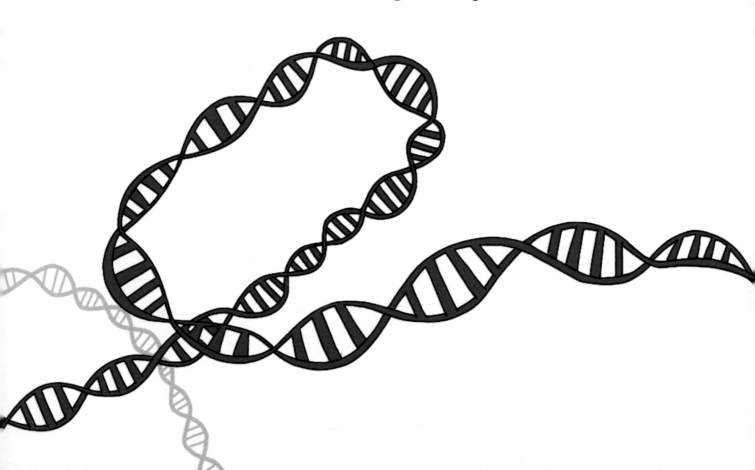

"Hello, Zoey," said a voice, and she turned around to see a woman standing behind her, smiling. "I'm Nettie Stevens, and I'm a scientist!"
"What's your story?" Zoey asked.

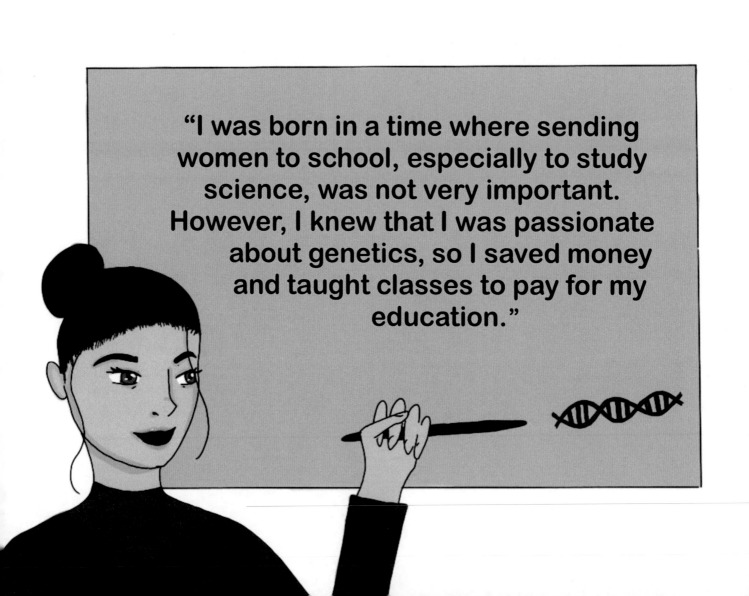

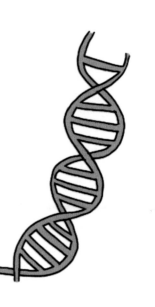

"During my time as a geneticist I made groundbreaking discoveries about whether someone is born as a boy or a girl by studying the cells of butterflies and other insects. At the same time, a man named Edmund Wilson made the same discovery, and even though my work had more evidence, I was largely overlooked. However, nowadays the world understands how people at the time might have trusted a man more, and I am remembered for my discoveries."

"Wow!" Zoey exclaimed, amazed at her story. "It's horrible you didn't get credit for your work, but it's good that now you get the recognition you deserve."
"If I had given up, I wouldn't have been able to pass on my knowledge to curious people like you!" Nettie smiled. I heard you had a wonder."

"I did." Zoey thought back to that morning. "I was looking at myself in the mirror and I began to wonder what makes people look unique. I know it's something called genes, but what are genes and how do they actually change what you look like?"

"That's a very good question." Nettie said. "In order to talk about genes, we're going to zoom way in on a living thing, so we can look at these things called cells, where DNA is stored. Everything that's alive, from me and you to a ladybug to a mushroom, are made up of lots of different kinds of cells, like building blocks."

"Cells have lots of different parts, but we're going to be focusing on a part in the center called the nucleus. The nucleus is like the brain or the control center for the cell-- it houses the DNA."

nucleus

"The DNA tells the cells what to do— tells them what type of cell they are, how big they need to be, even when to divide and make more cells! That's why red blood cells look so different than brain neurons-- they have different jobs, and the DNA makes sure they know what to do!"

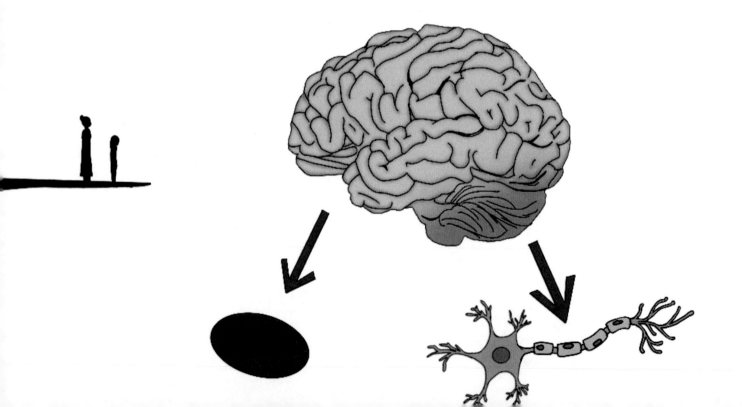

"That makes sense-- different cells have different jobs, so they need to look different. But what does the actual DNA look like? How does it work?" Zoey wanted to know.
"I'm glad you asked!" replied Nettie.

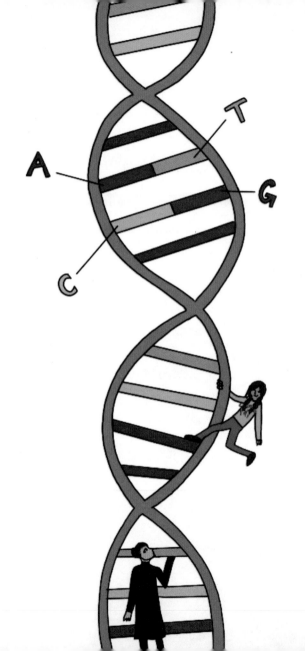

"DNA is shaped like a twisted ladder, also called a double helix. The rungs of that ladder are made up of four substances, called bases. The order that those four bases are in determines what the DNA tells the cell to do."

"Much of the DNA is useless, but certain patterns are important in telling cells to do certain things. These important sections are called genes, and small differences in the genes change how you look! For example, this pattern might cause someone to have blue eyes, and this one might cause someone to have brown eyes!"

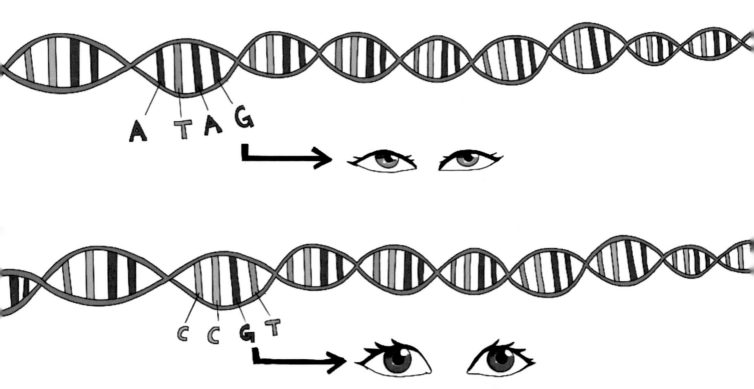

"Wow!" said Zoey. "I didn't know something that small could change something as big as someone's eye color!" She tried to imagine how it all fit together, but she realized something was missing. "So is the DNA just floating around in the nucleus?"
"That's a great question!" said Nettie.

"There is so much DNA inside each cell that it needs to be coiled and bunched together into structures called chromosomes. There are two types of chromosomes -- X chromosomes and Y chromosomes. Most humans have 46 chromosomes inside each nucleus but this is not the same for all living creatures— dogs have 76 chromosomes and potatoes have only 12."

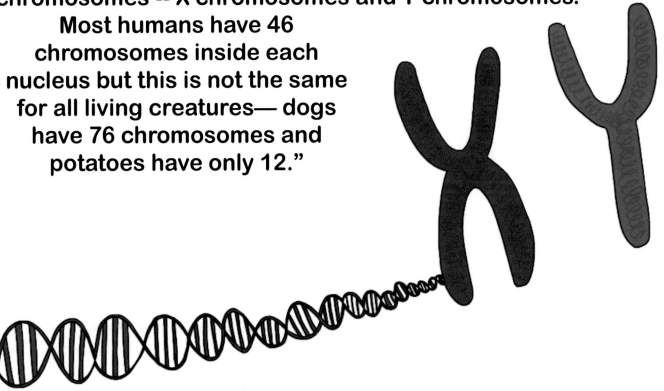

"Now, I know how important chromosomes are because that's where I did my research," Nettie said. "The shape of your chromosomes determines whether you are born as a boy or a girl -- girls have only X chromosomes and boys have both Y and X."

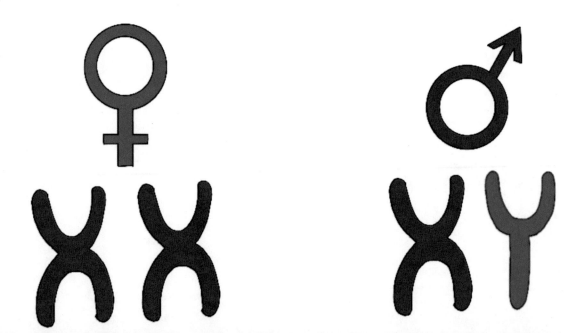

"Before my research, nobody knew what determined whether someone was born male or female. I discovered that it was linked to chromosomes through my experiments in insects. So to answer your question, chromosomes are the things floating around in the nucleus," she said with a wink.

"Genes are inside DNA which is inside chromosomes which are inside a nucleus in a cell!"
"That's making my head spin," admitted Zoey.
"It can be confusing." Nettie reassured her. "It took scientists years to figure out how DNA worked, and geneticists are making new discoveries to this day."

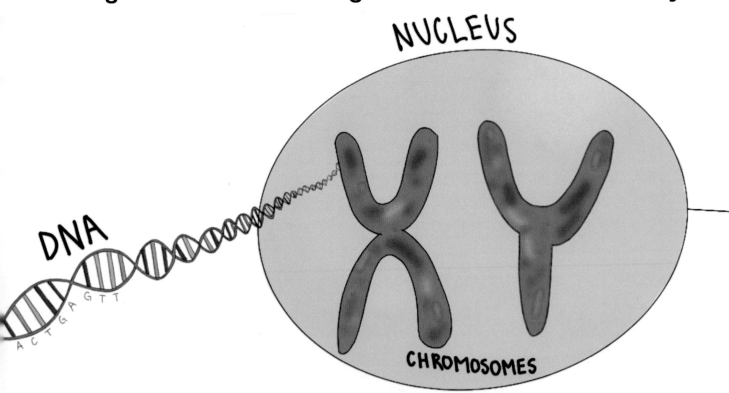

"Now that we know how DNA works, we can start talking about bigger ideas— like your wonder!"
"Yes!" said Zoey. She'd almost forgotten her wonder in all the excitement. "So why do we look like our parents?"

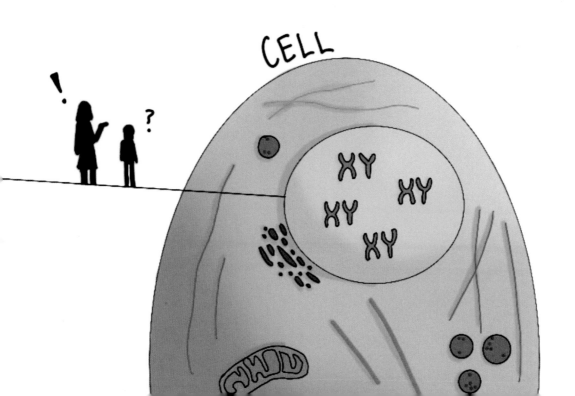

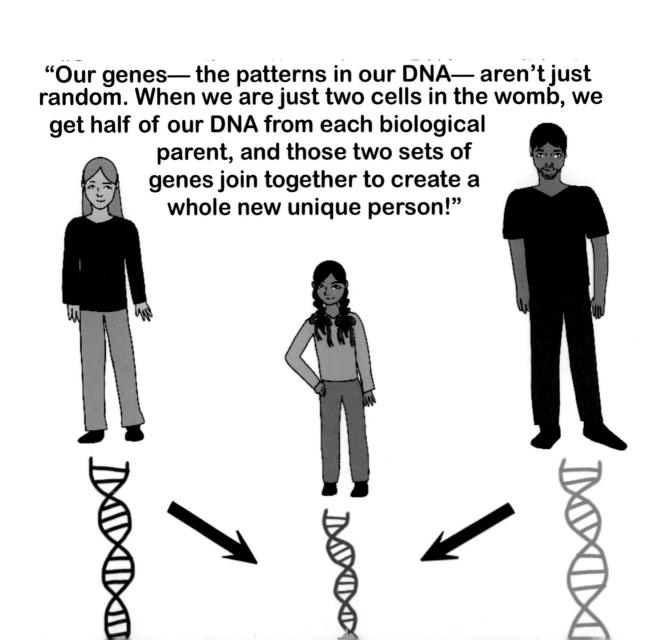

"Our genes— the patterns in our DNA— aren't just random. When we are just two cells in the womb, we get half of our DNA from each biological parent, and those two sets of genes join together to create a whole new unique person!"

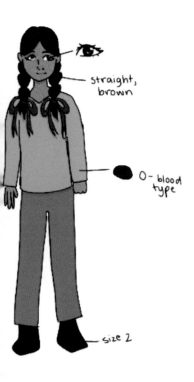

straight, brown

O- blood type

size 2

"The characteristics we inherit from our parents are called traits. Some of the more obvious ones are eye color, height, hair color or texture.

However, we also inherit traits we can't see such as diseases, blood types, and even liver function. We get half of our traits from each parent, since we get half of our DNA from each parent!"

Zoey thought about each of her parent's traits. People had always told her she looked much more like her dad -- she had dark hair like his, and his brown eyes. "If we inherit equal DNA, why do some people look much more like one parent?"
"Great question," Nettie said, "this is where it gets a little bit tricky."

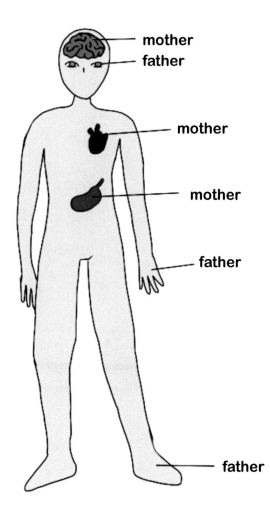

mother
father

mother

mother

father

father

"There are a couple reasons why someone might look much more like one parent," Nettie said. "The first is that the traits they inherit from one parent happen to be mostly non-visible ones, and the traits they inherit from the other parent are visible and obvious."

"Some traits are stronger than others, or they are more likely to show up in children. These traits are called dominant traits, and ones that are weaker or more rare are called recessive traits. Brown hair and brown eyes are both examples of dominant traits, so it's more likely you inherited them!"

Dominant	Recessive

"Wow!" said Zoey.

"There are many more dominant traits, such as dimples, curly hair, and even being able to roll your tongue, and lots of other recessive traits, such as short eyelashes, freckles, and blue eyes."

"Thank you!" said Zoey. "You answered my wonder, and now I know how DNA and genes work."
"Of course," said Nettie. "It's important to ask questions about what we see in the world around us. That's how great discoveries are made— by people who never stopped wondering." A warm smile, and Zoey faded into a peaceful sleep.

The next morning, Zoey woke up and as she was getting ready, she looked in the mirror the second time. As she looked at herself again, she was able to understand why she looked the way she did, and she was able to imagine what her genes looked like inside her cells.

At school, Zoey had an idea while eating lunch with some of her friends -- she wanted to test what she'd learned for herself. She asked them if they could roll their tongues. All of them could-- except one.

"I can't roll my tongue!" he exclaimed. "I wonder why that is?"

"Rolling your tongue is something called a recessive gene," Zoey explained excitedly. "It means most people can do it, but some people can't, and it's determined by your genetics before you're even born!"

"Wow!" he said. "How did you know that?"

And so Zoey said with a smile and a twinkle of knowledge in her eye, "I had a wonder."

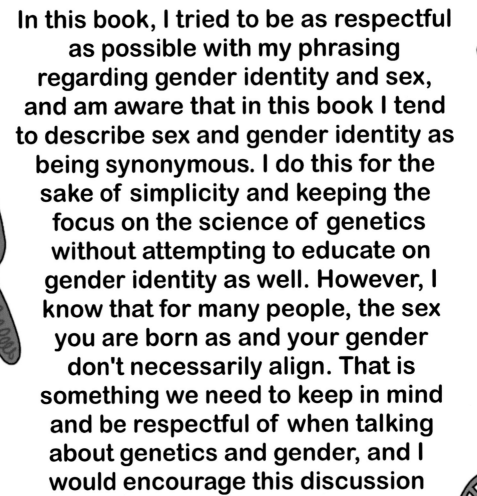

In this book, I tried to be as respectful as possible with my phrasing regarding gender identity and sex, and am aware that in this book I tend to describe sex and gender identity as being synonymous. I do this for the sake of simplicity and keeping the focus on the science of genetics without attempting to educate on gender identity as well. However, I know that for many people, the sex you are born as and your gender don't necessarily align. That is something we need to keep in mind and be respectful of when talking about genetics and gender, and I would encourage this discussion between parents and children before or after reading this book.

If you are interested, <u>Zoey Wonder: Exploring Reactions</u> is also available on amazon.com.

Thank you for reading!

Made in the USA
Las Vegas, NV
19 November 2021

34825271R00026